What We Inherit From Water

Yaffle's Nest Prize 2024

Introduction

I began swimming in cold water in 2020, during lockdown as a way of getting my head round what was happening in the world. The shock of the cold was like a restart and it helped me through the difficult times we faced. Of course, I started to write poems about the places where I swam and the difference it made to me and then I invited others to join me in workshops that celebrated water. Swimmers, non-swimmers, those who couldn't live without the icy shock of a winter river and those who dipped their toes in the sea once a year were all lured in by the promise of calm, of tingle, and sometimes the menace that water offered.

What we inherit from water means something different to all of us as the poems in this, Yaffle's Nest's first anthology show and whether you are a dipper, a diver, or a land-lubber, you're sure to find your inheritance here.

– Gill Connors – editor at Yaffle's Nest

Contents

First Prize
Gain access   Ian Harker   8
Second Prize
Rain   Holly Bars   9
Third Prize
William Walker saves
Winchester Cathedral   Jennifer A.
                                         McGowan   10

Highly Commended
Meltwater   Su Ryder   11
A Question for ...   Florence Ng   12
After swimming in the lido ...   Jason Conway   14
Leaving Shingle Street   Sue Butler   15

Commended
Brookside   Sharon Larkin   16
An extract from the journal ...   Sheila Jacob   17
Ammonite   Abigail Ottley   18
Water molecules   William
                                         Thirsk-Gaskill   19
The day she stops
being beautiful   Bobbie Sparrow   20
Yorkshire watter   Sally Brown   21

A glass of orange squash   Rachel Davies   22
Pissing myself   Patrick Druggan   23
A short day in Carlisle   Fokkina McDonnell   24
A squadron of tuna ...   Sandra Noel   25
A view from the future   Jenny Robb   26

Afraid	*Jill Lang*	27
An artic char's lament	*Bobbie Sparrow*	28
Blame it all on the weather	*Matt Nicholson*	29
Same shoes	*Gary Akroyde*	30
An Olympic length of life	*Jane Sharp*	31
And I	*Liz McPherson*	33
Circling the aquarium	*B.Anne Adriaens*	34
Astral swimming- ...	*Bruce Barnes*	35
Ball bouncers must pay	*Sue Butler*	36
River tales	*Fkorence Ng*	38
Climacteric	*Michelle Chew*	39
Confluence	*Sharon Phillips*	40
Crossing place	*Liz McPherson*	41
Dammed	*Louise J Jones*	42
Deflecting what		
never was straight line	*Sandra Noel*	43
elegy for a dead seal	*Sue Burge*	44
Morecambe Bay normal	*Sarah L Dixon*	45
Estuary	*Mary Anne*	
	Smith Sellen	46
This England	*Judi Sutherland*	48
Eve	*Sarah Graham*	49
Excalibur	*Ruth Higgins*	50
Fear of drowning ...	*Margaret Royall*	51
Flash floods	*Kathy Gee*	52
Headwaters of the Hull	*Tim Ellis*	53
River Mother	*Margaret Royall*	54
I find out on social media	*Lauren K Nixon*	55
Heart of the Potamoi	*Lauren K Nixon*	56
Heronry	*Mary Anne*	
	Smith Sellen	57
Pooled	*Julia Webb*	58
The Quiet One	*Maggie Mackay*	59

I took a walk once	Maggie Mackay	60
You won't remember the weatherman	Sharon Phillips	62
I'm not hoping for rescue at my age	Julie Elizabeth Griffiths	63
Flood warning	Judi Sutherland	64
In my water	Pat Edwards	65
Keeping out the cold	Linda Marshall	66
Learning	William Coniston	67
Lithium	Deborah Lyons	68
Melusine	Jennifer A. McGowan	69
Midsummer: dipping our toes in	Hannah Stone	70
Dunwich: February 2020	Sue Butler	71
My friend's cousin	Sue Mackrell	72
Naiad	Jennifer A. McGowan	73
By-Sea	Ali Murphy	74
Narrowboat	Damaris West	75
North Yorkshire steam train	Tonnie Richmond	76
Pond life	Kathy Gee	77
On Durham Heritage Coast	Sarah James	78
The Rigger	Abigail Ottley	80
Painting the Saltmarsh	Sue Burge	81
Pause for breath	Colin Day	82
Portrait of water	Kerry Darbishire	83
Night in the river	Josie Moon	84
Rain bright days	Patrick Druggan	85
River of salt	Rachael Clyne	86
Sea change	Cate Anderson	87
River watch	Patricia Leighton	88

Riverish	*Doryn Herbst*	90
Rivers of Heaven	*Gary Akroyde*	91
Wish you were here	*Sally Brown*	92
Spate	*Liz McPherson*	93
Send rain	*Lesley Quayle*	94
She is half in love with ink ...	*Abigail Ottley*	96
She went into the water	*Pat Edwards*	98
Standing on the ridge	*Patrick Druggan*	99
The field runs through your body	*Sandra Noel*	100
Sant Roma de Sau	*Judi Sutherland*	101
The journey to Gaza	*Jenny Robb*	102
The coastline below your house ...	*Sandra Noel*	103
Swimming with dolphins	*Ian Harker*	104
The Severn	*Louise Warren*	106
The river remembers	*Penny Blackburn*	107
The Tees	*Caroline Walling*	108
Turner's sketch of Kirkstall Abbey	*Clare Wigzell*	109
There you are again	*Christian Donovan*	110
Underwater	*Georgina Titmus*	111
Unseen	*Sarah Mnatzaganian*	112
Water pressure	*Elspeth McLean*	113
Wavelets	*Alwyn Marriage*	114
Globes	*Boakesey Closs*	115
So you can love her	*Rachel Glass*	116
Why swimming underwater ...	*Alison Jones*	118
The Watcher	*Helen Ivory*	119
Afterdrop	*Gill Connors*	120
Tregowris	*Mark Connors*	121
Savour the earth	*Nick Steel*	122

Gain access

If this was a painting it would be called
Golgotha: Hannen Heights.
The joiner is drilling the lock
and joking with the plumber about the smell
coming through the letterbox.

I am standing well back,
ready with my lanyard
and hoping that they've done a flit.
Hoping that the place is empty
and that the sink isn't backed up the same

as the washing machine that's leaking stale water
into the flat downstairs. That they've left the sofa
that was the only furniture anyway.
That they've binned the lighters and foils.
That there aren't a load of kids' toys piled up

behind the door and that there aren't two people
passed out in the bedroom. Two people who say
they never heard the braying on the door
or the drill screaming into the lock.
Two people who say they never read the letters

and that they don't feel the cold anyway. I'm hoping
that they've taken down the stained pink bedsheet
hung across the kitchen window, along with its pink light.
That one of them isn't standing naked on the stairs
screaming at me to get out of his fucking house.

Ian Harker

Rain

You've gone to sleep streaming digital rain from YouTube, and I'm left listening to the falling of it. It's different hearing rain and knowing that it will just keep going until you stop it. And this is how I take you for granted: you're as artificial as this rain because you're a people pleaser, wouldn't even admit to being freezing cold on our first date in the snow, wouldn't take the fresh pair of socks I offered you for your soaked feet. So now I think of you as some fixed thing which will hang around and never break up with me, and you'll gladly listen to this rain until it becomes water torture in your ears, and even after that. You always say *don't be daft* and give me a kiss, but I'm not being daft; maybe you're daft. Maybe you don't see how I can't read your fucking mind. Though all this thinking could just be a way I trick myself into believing I'm God of our situation, catastrophising a few drops of pretend rain into a downpour. I check where I'm at in my cycle for something to blame my thoughts on, then blame this bloody-shitting-rackety-bastarding YouTube rain, and all the women in films sitting in window boxes with fluffy socks, staring into their pathetic fallacy, a drill of water driving down any will to deviate from the heartbreak narrative. Bitches. I open my eyes and look at your face to get out of my own head. And I hate you for how perfect I think you are because it takes all my power. The rain noise continues to irritate me in the way it is a fantasy and smells of nothing, and has no claim to the stuff we're made of. Yet to get up and turn it off would mean having to move you, and you seem peaceful with your head on me whilst you sleep.

Holly Bars

Third Prize

William Walker saves Winchester Cathedral

Every day. Six years.
The deep dive into faith

into the septic, bone-ridden flood.
His suit fourteen stone, dry.
Wet, immeasurable.

And in the dark, to lay foundation
to the house above. The Itchen
wellspringing its hunger,
unruling the limestone blocks.

Twenty-five thousand bags of concrete.
Nine hundred thousand bricks.
How many *Hail Marys*?
How many *Oh Shits*?

How many sharp intakes of breath
on emerging and finding there was still a sun?

Jennifer A. McGowan

Meltwater

Metaphor for meltdown. Too much talk, too much presence is like three singer songwriters in one room. Dylan, Stipe, and Joel. Billy is starting *We Didn't Start the Fire*. As he trots out Harry Truman, Bob starts *Subterranean Homesick Blues*. Michael, meanwhile, launches his first line. *It's the End of The World as we Know it,* and *I Feel Fine*. It's patter protest slam, all of them simultaneously. Glorious, unholy trinity. Full, precision, and word-perfect rabbit. My brain, headlit, morphs into Raymond Babbit, with Charlie hounding him onto a plane. Clenching and hollering, again, again, superglued synapses, melding and welding swelled tissues of sick and smouldering brain. Put me to simmer outdoors, with an ice-clinking glass of what I'm seven-tenths made of. Run it slowly through the babbling lips. Lubricate the jammed machinery. Turn molten tissue from white hot to stainless, neutralising crisis into painless. Angel Falls, the Nile, pushing through lava to quench spewing, sore, mortified Chernobyl of the core. The music changes its frenetic tempo. Crescendo softens to andante and lento. Sure, whatever isn't water here will always be burning. But she's *Always a Woman*. Peace, *Lay, Lady, Lay*. I am *At My Most Beautiful* diluted. Meltwater will wash meltdown away.

Su Ryder

A Question for the Freedom Swimmers of the 60's

What if
against
bullets
against
typhoon
against
barking dogs
against
torchlight
against
a slip off a cliff
against
waves
seeing nothing
feeling nothing
waves
against
sharks
against
six hours like this
you find you land

but a street away
you know
don't you
and I, from now, can assure you
it's a colossal bamboo theatre
someone takes you in
offers you clothes
a job
speaking your language

Highly Commended

their acting so good
everyone's acting so hard
for the place to become real
a girl smiles at you
a magnolia opens at night
you don't have to worry
she'll tell on you
will you still
seriously prepare
and dare death?

Florence Ng

After swimming in the Lido, Father, I thought of you leaving

Neurons fire in a white waving mesh on a light blue floor,
   as praying hands
search for the dry sun & glass is blown in amorphic
   sculptures which rise,
then vanish as if they never were, recalled in bubbles inside
   my mind.

Under the surface, all is muted & yet, in constant change:
   of pattern, shade,
movement & the dance of light, as spheres of breath
   ascend. Feet kick, hands
push, bodies glide & minds focus on the immediacy of
   motion from wall,

through water, to wall. Fingers & toes sense waters flow as
   hair undulates
to its cool stroke of silver rhythm & I rock like a baby in a
   weightless cradle,
as though sway is a meditation to regress to the womb of a
   world within

a world, where existence was simple & snug, with no pain,
   fear, cry or gasp
but this place is like the cycle of birth to death & all that is
   in between is flux.
Filled with the bond of air & heart & I wish for more time
   here to watch

Jason Conway

Leaving Shingle Street

Six tide-turns notice they were given
to leave. They took their big bed
that came to them when Granddad Church died.

It drizzled and the sheets went damp onto the cart.
The Harbour Inn would be target practice,
direct hits blasting gouts of stale beer
across the beach, into the dead end of the lane.

Still the restless sea shoves at the shingle.
The lazy wind cuts to bone.
It's just stuff my cousin says.
A week is enough. So we sit by her bed
and talk of the weather and wait.

Sue Butler

Brookside

Hazel catkins drizzle pollen by the weir. The brook breaks the ice, spills her gravy over, laps cow-churned lips. Spring holds its breath. Listen. In the hush, a vole plops, glides, and wakes the water. A wood-pecker drills in an ash tree. Celandines sun themselves in the water-meadow while violets cower on the bank, flinching from new-sprung nettles. Ladies' smocks lure fools to the marsh. Blind to hungry pike below, willows drool new leaves over eddies. Flags and reeds set the stage for damsels to dance. On cue, a kingfisher sparks, breaks the mirror, flaunts a stickleback. Before long, rosebay willowherb sets torches blazing. Teasels taunt the elder, mourning her berries. Her yellowed spears miscarry in a torrent and are sluiced away. From reed beds, geese racket up and skein off against a dying sun, fungus blurts from a stricken trunk, and the moon looks on as her twin lies cracked in a backwater. Somewhere a gudgeon gulps. Brittle twigs twitch in the blizzard, a lonely haw hangs grimly on and moorhens perish as the brook pulls on her lace.

Sharon Larkin

An extract from the journal of Miss Jane Fairfax
After *Emma* by Jane Austen

Mr George Knightly suspects – frowned, when Frank
retrieved my shawl, placed it around my shoulders. What
shall I say if he quizzes me?
Simply that Weymouth bewitched us.
Leaves were changing colour, gambolled through fish-
tanged streets. The breeze spun my skirts, wrapped muslin
between my thighs.
The tide's crescendo almost stopped my breath, powered
Frank's words.
I confess, Miss Fairfax, I feel more alive near the sea. Such
openness, such wildness.
I watched him skim flat stones across the waves, saw the
glint of hairs on his wrist.
The sand was damp beneath my feet, the tops of my
stockings moist, warm.
We contrived to be alone on our last evening, resolved,
then, on a secret engagement, before he returned to
Yorkshire and I travelled back to London.
He fingered the buttons of my pelisse, pressed his lips to
the hollow of my throat while the sun crumbled like
burning coals.
Gulls swooped onto the water, scooped salt air into their
throats, breathed it over the harbour in raucous song.

Sheila Jacob

Ammonite
(Mollusca Cephalopoda)

the hidden one
hard to pin down
like the horned god
you were named for

snake-stone embedded in
grim northern rock
serpent left to speak in tongues

tiger-striped and spiralling
seeds within seeds
sperm-shapes swimming
in your chambers

house and home to
a mollusc gone missing

nautilus undone.

Abigail Ottley

Water molecules

Each one is a little, spiky thing,
looking like something the police
might scatter on the road to burst the tyres
of a stolen car. They are in the exhaust
emitted by the car. They are in the exhaust
emitted every time you exhale.

They suffer from bipolarity and are
sick beyond treatment, unable even to admit
they have a problem.
This condition makes them stick to their neighbours,
faster than leeches,
faster than Triads, the Mafia:
faster than that chap you met at the freshers' fair
who had seemed all right at first.
Sixty per cent of him was made of them.
They were trying to stick to you then, like they
are sticking together now, inside you,
in your blood, your guts, your brain.

If it weren't for the insane grip
of these little tetrahedrons,
there'd have been no Pyramids,
no Hitler, no Internet, no mobile phones,
nothing carved into the Stanza Stones.

William-Thirsk Gaskill

The day she stops being beautiful

She picks her way through coralline,
    pauses while the horizon fades on
Trá an Dólín, her bare feet are blue.
    Waves diminish like hands receding
their gifts, each calico froth unwraps
    the sand, heavy with the ocean's weight.

Her dress feels like it must be shed,
    now she is invisible, it is a shroud.
She is Venus at night, the museum steward's
    footsteps are forged in sand, he hums
as he dusts her face, covers her body.
    He does not look into her eyes anymore.

The night sky appears like a stage curtain,
    navy-velvet, heavy with stars made by men.
There is no encore, she will not sing again,
    her voice was interrupted by loss, she cannot
recall the lyrics and the audience is gone.
    She curls herself like an empty nautilus.

Fifty per cent water, point four per cent salt,
forty-four point six percent grief.

Bobbie Sparrow

Yorkshire watter
after Jean Sprackland

Tha's soft int' head.
Must be all that Yorkshire watter tha've
swallowed,
standing at bus stop int' rain,
at all times of day.
Dunt tha know last bus never runs?
Aye. Soft as a brush.

Anno what tha's gonna say
but don't try stoppin it in its tracks.
It'll take thee out with a Saturday night
punch,
drag tha through t'mill wheels
and spin tha
flat as a farrier's cap.

And when it pours
tha'll know about it.
Seepin intut seams of tha skin,
braying tha wi 'orizontal bucketfuls,
until tha coat weighs a chuffin' tonne
and tha hair's like weeds down a wet dam wall.

And all those 'eee bah gum' farmers
strokin their manky beards
and leaning ont'walls,
tryin to measure t'weather with their
thumb.
Watchint' clouds
like dumb-struck beasts.

'appen mehbe that's why we say
'reyt as rain'
when folks ask how we're doin.   *Sally Brown*

A glass of orange squash

The water in my orange squash
fell as rain, puddled, evaporated,
collected and cooled in clouds,
outweighed the cloud's ability
to hold it, fell as rain.
Precipitation, evaporation,
condensation, gravity:
the cycle on repeat.

My orange squash is diluted by
the same water tikktaalik
and coelacanth climbed out of
to breath air on dry land;
the same water terrorised
by the fearsome pliosaur,
sea god of the Jurassic Coast.

My orange squash is diluted by
Noah's storm, St Swithin's curse,
diplodocus drink, pterodactyl piss.
That's the water cycle is,
that's what I'm drinking.
Nothing changes.

Rachel Davies

Pissing myself

An adult mammal
empties its bladder
in twenty seconds,

enough time for you
to read to the end
of this short sentence.

Patrick Druggan

A short day in Carlisle

I was the nearest
subcontractor, hired hand
for the firm in Epsom.

The Environment Agency
had booked them
to provide a counsellor.

The underpass still closed,
dark brick walls of the Fire Station,
buses and fire engines drying out.

An older man ambled in.
I gave him the leaflet of what
to do with a post-flood garden.

Keep all photos, videos,
all items with sentimental value
safe, up on the first floor.

Fokkina McDonnell

A squadron of tuna are lifting the sea out of itself

This drama of white thrash
reminds me of Aunt Mary's frenzied sleep-runs
under the covers; her knees laddering up and down,
forever trying to reach Bill in the fire.

As suddenly as they erupted
the tuna swim away, mackerel full.
The sea belches back through its door,
sinks to sleep in flat sheets.

When Mary and her night legs died,
her duvet was laid to rest.

Sandra Noel

A view from the future

She's glad she lives on a hill,
though arthritis hobbles her radius
and the incline to fields
at the back now defeats her.

Deprived of field snowdrops,
she plants bulbs in pots,
rejoices at their will
to live again each year.

Down the hill, Otterspool prom
no longer throngs with dog walkers
and cyclists. She hears it's crumbled,
lost its battle with the Mersey.

But the wetlands are welcome.
Bitterns boom and sphagnum moss
is making a comeback. So far
the river has failed to isolate

her hill, and she's grateful for warmth.
Heating bills no longer terrorise.
This year, her ninetieth,
snowdrops stay buried.

Jenny Robb

Afraid

There is no sea fret, just mother
pacing the shoreline while we paddle,
Atlantic kissing our ankles.

We tell her not to worry, we like
the ocean, the salt, want to splash
and swim till our skin turns blue.

Her lips don't move yet we
hear her careful pleas ripple
round the bay and back.

We try to stay close, arms
perform gentle breaststroke, feet
walk the sand beneath till water lifts us.

She rarely comes in, scared. We know
that's why she never showers. She says
it's like drowning, makes her gasp for air.

Jill Lang

An artic char's lament

I swim in the rhythm of salty waves
lifting my belly in melodic rubato.
Pickle coloured seaweed floats,
slides across my shine.

I bear the weather, my body an instrument
beneath whimsical clouds.
Twenty-five knots, gusting to thirty-four,
showery troughs increasing rough, rise rapidly.

Malin Head to Carnsore Point
I am the trumpet blown,
the tempest of a bassoon.
I flirt with sardines, circles of piccolos.

I am a creature in decline, my music dims.
Confused by man's debris, his noise,
my rhythm eludes me; I lose time
where once there was none.

The clash of swells and storms
wash out my map, eyes now see
only orange twists, bobbing grey bottles,
blue rope entwined with dirty cloth.

Pressure rises, squalls chant.
Plastic is netting without purpose,
caught like a note in the tenor's throat.
I am an Arctic Char, my only song now a lament.

Bobbie Sparrow

Blame it all on the weather

It wasn't rain that evacuated the sky
disowned the clouds and struck the ground

It wasn't rain that caused the rivers to swell
to eat up the villages and towns

It wasn't rain that grew like an uprising
and pulled the city walls down

It wasn't rain – rain was just for context
it was you who let everybody drown

Matt Nicholson

Same shoes

We parted
on the banks of the muddy Calder,
our shoes thick with Yorkshire clay.

I left the gurning cloughs and sad, grey hills,
strangling villages and scratchy air.

Danced the path of Incas to blooms of passion fruit,
saw diamond waterfalls in the Cloud Forest river,
sipped volcanic starlight through the heart of a Quito
moon,
and watched purple sunsets sweep sands of Cartagena.
Followed the trail of Sundance over dusty Tupiza plains,
Supped with fútbol scholars in bars of Buenos Aries,
whirled my way sloshed to Santiago
and its burgundy bruised rains.

Back to the grinning Calder valley
with its swirling, emerald hills;
liquid villages and crystal frosted air.

Tattooed with feverish memories,
incantations bleeding from my eyes.

You stared past me,
entrenched in Leeds
on the pub telly,

wearing those
same muddy shoes.

Gary Akroyde

An Olympic length of life

In the pool up to her neck in water,
her arms stretched out in front, she casts off, moves

fishlike, into the blue, sucking up her
life with every gulp of air. Ripples

mandala the otherwise still surface,
as she swims towards the deep end, frog-feet

and paddle-palms pushing her determined
body through the shark-less way ahead. She

swallows her childhood, allows lost play days
to fill her belly with blind innocence,

gobbles her adolescence, exhales fears,
paranormal ideas, penis dreams,

menstrual dreads, thoughts of Hell. She digests
her hallucinations, enriches her

blood with the nutrients of sin, takes a
mouthful of achievements and strengthens her

bones with the weight of well-chewed wins. She blows
a hole in the water, a hole full of

fist-clenched repression. Ripples radiate
until they lick the overflow, cause waves.

She tastes motherhood like a pro, trusting
her instinct to keep afloat, kicks her legs,

makes her arms work, pushes on. The ripples
momentarily becoming whipped flotsam

as she changes position, floats on her
back, takes a deep breath and consumes heartbreak.

Satisfied, her sight on the long course, she
crawls home. Her fingers touch tile; she makes it

to the other side, re-energized. Dries
off. Allows life to settle in her gut –

the after-dinner armchair – her thoughts
already on her next Olympic length.

Jane Sharp

And I   pulled from
the flood   five
sheep   and   four
head of cattle the
young   bullock
being   swept
down river   I never
thought   to see
him again   gale an
express train   flung
in our faces   seabed
carried   to moors
crane   ripped from
its place   back
broken on   the iron
bridge   all those
man-made   things
carcasses   of   trees
but   the young
bull was   found
after   rapids   and
waterfall   flung
hoof over   head
wind   humming
like a wire   down
the valley   till he
came at last   to his
feet   both of
us   humbled

Liz McPherson

Circling the aquarium

It wasn't a god who scooped out fractions of ocean
to pour them into the largest fishbowl. And it wasn't you
who raised a solid membrane between two realms.

You're but one mammal among many, trudge
from one ecosystem to the next then circle back,
loudness of children at the periphery of perception.

Subliminal whispers inside your cranium tell you
to plonk yourself on the floor, shoulder to the partition.
Catch the eye of stingrays, sharks and all the others

you don't have a name for, as they brush against the glass
like cats against your hand, circling back for more,
a gentle current through the water crossing

the boundary cooling your palm. Breathe on this side;
hear them sigh on the other. This may be enough
to feed a dream of unimpeded movement:

a submarine without a hull, on land and yet submersed,
you join this circular ballet and share the illusion
of a giant wave that would set them free.

B.Anne Adriaens

Astral Swimming-in memoriam Manningham Baths 1903-2012-

'In water, all possibilities seemed infinitely extended':
Roger Deakin, *Waterlog*

I swim against restraint and the soak of the old,
breast stroking passed depths written in half measures;
the 1903 Baths Committee commemorative stone
lifeguards poolside. By the spittoon I've never used
I drop my head, keeping the bridge of the nose
as a plimsoll line and feel watery limbs
stroking, gently, quietly, at their element.
Skylight sun picks out a horizon of white
edge tiles, burnishing them to a thread that plays
me in, lands me in the roof girders' cage.

The cubicles are empty, curtains flung back
over their rails; water ripples in turquoise
swim lanes, whipping the tiled markers to lassos.
The side windows reflect wiggling squares of light
to dive through. I'm shocked at my below par progress:
the left leg screw-kick, a divergent arm pull,
trunks that sag below the waist, teenage style.
But then it wouldn't be me, watching me touch
the grab rail, swivel then fold the knees for push off...

to swim a roof space length, mock water spurting
through my breathing, passed rusting ventilators,
the dentil moulding in yellow brick, and the notice
beyond which non swimmers shouldn't go.
I do, anticipating my body, feeling the shell
for what it mostly is: two parts hydrogen,
one part oxygen, and the third element
no one knows yet. I surface by the shallows
finding that entirety- switch to an inept
stroke, a splashing and noisy crawl.

Bruce Barnes

Ball bouncers must pay

for balls they bounce/ make you want to bounce one/ feel in
your feet the hard inelastic plastic smack the pavement/
bang/ sassy as a teenager/ bang/ who abuses while he
smiles/ bouncing/ see/ bouncing/ bang/ a half-dozen balls/
fag end of summer dull/ thumb-smeared as the note tied to
their cage/
skip divers might recycle them/
fenders for ferries/   floats for mussel lines/
bounces small/ as the waves beneath the harbour wall/
faded/ neon pink/ baby blue/
they'll appear on postcards/

The view from our favourite café. Wish you were here.

strung together/

into the sky

                                and away/
                                   up the hills/
        they'll lead the eye down the loch/

There is no away for plastic/ weathered hard and brittle/
their twine ties perished /

        they'll drift   rise on the waves
                on the tide   be
dashed
                           against gneiss
and sandstone boulders

        on the beach

                              rise

                                        and   be
dashed

                                        shatter

              against

                                                  the
billion year wisdom

                                                  of
Lewisian

                                                  and
Torridonian
                    slowly ground

                                    to pink

                                              and blue
                            dust

the prettiest extinction layer on the planet

                                        Sue Butler

37

River tales

It was not until corpse
after corpse streamed down the river
that the Hong Kong Government knew
there were massacres in mainland villages.

It was so small
we could actually walk across it.
The faces of customs officers changed
from civil to ill-tempered Justice Bao;
their uniform from navy blue to toad green.

On the Hong Kong side the Sandy Ridge Cemetery.
A number for each unclaimed body
to be exhumed and cremated every 7 years.
Even the numbers will be replaced
by the year when their ashes are gathered in a square
under one headstone.

Don't buy things from street vendors.
The bag of herbs could be hay.
Don't run away from parents.
See the limbless beggars?
You want to be one?

Florence Ng

Climacteric*

like Venus enduring her solar fall
we are losing water –

what singular life did she transfigure
    in secret
as her ichorous self evanesced

weeping vapours in high winds
bequeathing ancient memory in burning bones

ekpyrosis-in-waiting
every drop beloved
wasting nothing
    more.

Michelle Chew

*also Menopause

Confluence

but as for

the Trym

it don't amount to much

piddling little stream

silted up by runoff

from shopping malls

and car parks

tributaries shrivelled

busy port

gone

the harbour walls and docks

taverns and cobbled yards

to-and-fro of boats

trade in wool and silver

speculatores on the prowl

it skulks in culverts

sidles past

back gardens

dribbles

into

Avon's

mud

Sharon Phillips

Crossing place

i

You bring me hawk-shadowed moorland, silvered falls, deer-mottled forests, you sing of The Strid, sliding its greasy depths past bones and bones to shingled stepping stones, over sticklebacks flicking in dappled shallows, reeding of moorhens, imperious swans. And I, having only the dust of feet, oily pneumatics of axles and engine-roar, tacky ice-creamed fingers, pointless chatter. It belongs to you for an instant but is my every hour. Today in April sunshine you're in good humour, and I'm glad of that. But sometimes I long for you to take me past pleasure boats and playground to the wide oxbow of the beach, whatever lies beyond.

ii

The oxbow is my next unknown, pulled as I am by something all unloosed. Call it impatience, adventure, the roar of the wild but see how they vanish, the places, the faces, how they run between my restless fingers nothing ever fixed, nothing remaining in my endlessness and you, already a faint echo of what once was. You are the perpendicular, marking time, fastened and everything coming to you.

Liz McPherson

Dammed

A band of concrete thrown broad across
a flattened weir, a thousand times as high.
The sun, spliced by silica and lime,
no longer lands on the erased, worm-lazy riverbank.

How to get your head around what's held back;
a small ocean, piped sweet and fast
to all our taps. Harnessed muscle
till wicket gates gape; unleash its clout.

This water lying cradled in the air awaits its man-made
fate; but first it plays with secret swimmers
who splash and spool around its spillways
and morning-glory pools.

Louise J Jones

Deflecting what never was straight line

You hold the bones of me so we can hold on;
tell me we will make it through tomorrow
and tomorrow, our child will be ok.

I wish Dad was here to read these clouds
that are eating each other, show me how
to keep cool in this pressure cooker with no vent.

You say the tide's a revolving door;
different water will soon pull up the sun.
They will see this is not our doing.

Tonight, we allow our waters to boil over
under the deep of it all.

Sandra Noel

elegy for a dead seal

like a broken   sonnet
octave: part flesh & flipper
  gull-ripped-raggèd
        then the lyric turn to picked bone
sestet of curved & salted spine
        skull empty of little wild words   just learnt

i don't want to swim today
  put my face close to the fading
        thump & throb of cells
          the tide peels from his body
as it turns   a ceaseless volta
    a smell of   what?   something more alive than
death
                something that brings to mind a butcher's
hook

& pink   too much pink

Sue Burge

Morecambe Bay normal

That hug.
The first I have had from anyone not my son,
for three months.
I didn't want to step away from it,
held on.
A foot taller than me.
You felt my need to be held.

We walk along to the Morecambe Tandoori.
We don't wear masks, though I have mine in my hand.
Seated in the window, so I can watch the sea,
The shore, where I spent the afternoon
stroking circles into sand,
lifting sea-glass, testing for sharp edges
and storing the smooth ones in mint-tins,
to take home.

You order with ease.
I can tell you eat out more often than I do.
You choose sides to share.
You tell me the meal is on you.

You pour out wine into glasses.
I don't know when I last had wine
from a glass laid out on a tablecloth,
toasted positive things,
talked of the future
as if it was something
I could see again.

Sarah L Dixon

Estuary

I am the Thames and when I speak to the sea
                                                                    the sea listens

where the Swale is shifting in its bed of London clay   between
salt marsh
        and the isle's upturned hulk out as far as the hovering
arrays
of white-winged angels ghostly ships and flickering forts

where cloud-streets tumesce into towering temples
        and the sun tips slowly beyond the hazed horizon
this is where I speak of all I 've carried   the living and the
dead

paupers and kings exiles and idlers toilers innocent and
damned
        the fractured reflections of sun moon and stars the
bloom
and the bruise of sky and clouds refracted in vitreous light

all of you are just passage migrants fleeting glimpses in
eternity's time-lapse
        but you and your memories I will hold forever
no one can ever own me but I will always own you

when you have dissolved into uniform dust I can still flesh
you out
        in each grey mote and glassy grain I retain the
knowledge of dermis and bone
tissue ligament sinew and muscle the helix of hair I honour
the legacy
of hollowed womb sated sacs slaked breasts the born and the
unborn
        your sweat breath and tears are taken up into the
altocumulus

of a chaotic sky I reflect on your eyes in the changing hues of
water and light

your kisses are locked in the salt-tanged spray your raised
voices given
        to the unmuted Swans all your whispers to the hissing
reeds
Oystercatchers snatch away your children's laughter your
unanswered

questions consigned to the Curlews your sunlight is stashed
        in the Yellow-Horned Poppy the moon in the Barn
Owl's face your grey days
buried in the Great Heron's feathers spring swathed in Sea
Lavender

and summer snapped in the wings of Common Blues your
autumns
        glow in the Golden Samphire winters linger in Egrets
and Gulls
your sunsets burn in the breasts of Mergansers your nights'

noctilucence in the Cormorant's embrace your storms all
mirrored in the rough
        roaring waves contentment tucked under linenfold calm
secrets buried
in the mudflats' clasp thoughts encrypted in the scribble of
the sand

I am the Thames and when I to speak to the sea
                                        the sea listens
        reassuringly retreats
returns   and remembers   the unfathomable weight
                                        of my
waterborne words

                              Mary Anne Smith Sellen

This England

I remember all the places that have gone,
sunk under waves, salted and slack
where now the country rests beneath the tides,
the drowned face of the earth which the water tracks
like tears. A wasting grace, a Lyonesse
a second Doggerland. If this reality
is a dream, I've been dreaming it too long.
Big crows still sit cawing on bare trees
on branches too gentle for their weight -
a poor fanfare for the Fisher King, seized
like his kingdom, unfit for habitation.
This island, this England. Into the maritime.

Judi Sutherland

Eve

We all began here –
our journey from single cells
to complex beings,
bathed in the all-encompassing
womb of the sea.
A sometimes benevolent
mother, caring and nurturing,
nourishing her water babies,
keeping them from harm.

But sometimes cruel –
expelling shellfish on
the shore, twice a day.
Cast out like naughty children,
shattered and scattered.
Providing fodder for
scavenging gulls and crows.

She takes some of it back,
cleaning the beach,
scouring and bleaching
the empty shells - some shiny,
some as thin as paper.

Sarah Graham

Excalibur

In the back of the locked car
      you attempt escape — you escape
            to do something with the wildness inside.

When your father was a child they'd say
      Go and jump in the lake!
            and you did, on a hot August day

in the black leather jacket
      you wouldn't take off all that summer
            when you were half wild cat

half Marlon Brando so cool
      and we were the hot stained road you pounded
            looking for ways through

thickets of thorn and mistake we had planted
      until I saw you emerge clear-eyed again,
            dripping light, your jacket in shreds.

Ruth Higgins

Fear of drowning replays in a childhood nightmare

Stand still! Look how the sea is drawn to you;
dark magnetism pulls you closer in,
and you would wade in deep in socks and shoes,
replay once more that haunting childhood scene:
a drowning man. *Act now, girl, pull him out!*
The tide turns, sweeps him back, he can't push on
Your mother sleeps, the coastguard's on a shout,
*the lifeguard clocked off early... **You're the one!***

I was a child, afraid, too mute to scream,
though storms clouds loomed and death was imminent.
Was this reality, or just a dream?
A ten year old the only saviour sent?

Desist! There's nothing more that could be done -
Forgiveness is not needed   life moves on.

Margaret Royall

Flash floods

Our confluence is swept aside
as if our footprints
cannot bear to walk together.

Icy currents deepen, surge
where friendship can't survive
a further freezing.

Over time, we meet in clearings,
celebrate their placid waters,
building bridges out of debris.

Then the mountain sends
another flood, another parting.
Hope lets out a sigh and dies.

Kathy Gee

Headwaters of the Hull

They thrilled me, child with open eyes, the trout
that loafed here as I leaned out from the bridge.
They loiter to this day, as though throughout
my years they haven't aged. I loved their thorough
stillness, how the current couldn't budge
them from the chalk stream bed by any terror
then - back then - with Mum and Dad and Gran,
the Hull's headwaters clear and no one gone
downriver yet, when bliss was but to sit
forever staring. Now, despite my cautious
inch, with rapid tail-fin flicks they split,
depart this spot from where my happiness spilt
when I leaned out before the lucid waters
slowed their flow and soured, then fugged with silt.

Tim Ellis

River Mother

River mother sings
to the crooked quercus,
to windswept fields
burnished with toppled cornstooks,
ululates the seductive hum
of pagan summers.

She whispers to
penumbras of wood sprites,
to star watchmen blowing
on frozen fingers,
murmurs to the wastelands
of ice-barbed winters.

Life-giver, life-taker,
sustainer of the foetus in the womb,
the blossoming of flora and fauna,
her credentials impeccable.

She is a wise crone,
mirroring our *humanitas*
tracing life from cradle to grave;
between source and delta
an instinctive ritual,
playing out from vaults of deep time.

Margaret Royall

I find out on social media

that's how I get most news these days
trapped, as we all are, in small labyrinths

fortified against the contagion at the gate

I draw a bath, throw in petals and herbs
grab the bottle of wine from the fridge
and message Christine about your loveliness

together - apart - we giggle and weep

just last week, we were talking harps
and folk songs, full of the old stories you love
now you're not just distant, but absent

the phantom of your last, rattling breath
haunts the bathroom, hiding behind the towels
peeking out from under the soap

I reread your ghost story, then it hits me

the relief that our work could collide just once
before we knew there wouldn't be a second chance

I stay in the bath until my fingers wrinkle
toasting a friend, water turning salty
your last rites, rinsed clean

Lauren K Nixon

Heart of the Potamoi

a stone drops

ripples spread and break, disturbing the thing that lies
beneath
bubbles form, chaos spreads

She rises, rubbing coal-dark eyes to look upon the world
tilting her head to listen to the cries on the wind

She does not like what she finds
She rises, and rises again
Tethys, stirring her rivers into flood

it is time for the spear and the shield,
it is time to be terrible

Lauren K Nixon

Heronry

A steely blade pinning lake to landscape,
a sniper, grey-cloaked and hunched.
The reed-like reflection of his bayonet bill
a decoy for a dagger that swiftly splits
the water's skin, eviscerates
a twist of molten silver.

How marvellous the moment
of his considered ascent as he leans
into the breeze, rounded wings scooping air.
Needle-like, he bears the storm's calm eye
through the chaos of clouds
in a slow, measured progress.

He parallels the horizon with a trail
of ruddered legs, full-sails the sky,
before his gentle descent towards distant trees.

Feet now lowered,

he meets the sanctuary of sticks
where sits the tableau of his brood -
a quiver of freshly-fletched arrows,
tensing as one at his approach.

How monumental that they already know
what we have yet to learn:
stillness as a strategy for survival,
and how deadly a weapon just waiting can be
when wielded with dignity, and in silence.

Mary Anne Smith Sellen

Pooled

there's a woman on the side
windmilling her arms
there are girls with their pony tails

and Little Mermaid armbands
and a woman who sinks down carefully
into the folds of herself

but here come the shouting men
arms like bent umbrella spokes
mouths like broken pots

even underwater you hear can them
their mouths like tunnels
hoovering up the light

the women cluster together
knotting themselves into a fist
making a wall around the girls

while the men expand to fill the space
the bad spouting out of them
into the chemical water

Julia Webb

The Quiet One
After Seurat's The Bathers of Asnières

He's hemmed in, the boy
with the hunched shoulders
gazing at the water,
a liquid of death.

Somehow
he has to prove himself,
to belong, to carry on.

They tried it on before
when he started work
in that vile factory.

First time, all four of them
grabbed legs and arms,
dog snarling, as he kicked.

That splash,
body hitting the surface,
the gobbling and spluttering,
their garbled laughter
as he pushed towards air.

His feet never touched silt or stone,
body flailing like a hooked perch
or pike, more like.

In the stillness of Sunday afternoon heat
he's fighting fit – secret boxing classes.
The one in the bowler hat has
to be watched. Ringleader. Bully.

Maggie Mackay

I took a walk once

from the towpath to the edge of the Roman Empire at
Antony's Wall, most complex barrier they ever built, where
once columns of centurions marched. Laden supply carts
and oxen, horses and watchtowers. Heading to Auntie
Katie's Inn where boatmen supped and chortled. Men from
Leith, Hull, Hamburg heading for Glasgow where the Union
Canal joins the Forth and Clyde Canal. Two Carved faces -
Greetin and Laughin- , the boom of blasting tunnels. To
Polmont, where serious school boys sported on grounds by
the canal, boxed and played rugby. A landing stage and a
footbridge still remain. Pit workers toiled further along the
canal. I reached Woodcockdale's honeyed stables, the smell
of hay and grain. The voices of grooms and passengers
talking fares and the speediest barges. There was bustle, as
horses rested or were changed. Their hooves clicked, manes
shook. I stopped where the Pardovan cist was discovered.
Bronze Age folk interred one of their own, then through
Hopetoun Woods. Towards Dougal's brickworks and
Cobbinshaw Reservoir which services the canal. Lin's mill,
named after William Lin, owner of a nearby mill who
became the last person in Scotland to die of the 1645 plague.
I looked out for stage markers, took a breather at Bridge Inn
where horses were rested and stabled at Change House. So
many inns for thirsty bargemen. They drank nearby at Pop
Inn, entering by one door and leaving on the canal side..
They caught up with their vessel as the horses pulled along
the towpath. I hear their hobnail boots clacking on cobbles.
Edging towards Edinburgh I crossed Slateford Aqueduct.
The smell of hops grew. Close by, Fountain Brewery. The
Leamington Lift Bridge moved three times along the canal.
The North British Rubber Works stood in all its imperial

glory. Not far from my childhood home, its stone villa built for the manager. Lochrin Basin, the terminal. Modern conference centres and hotels, leisure parks. Port Hopetoun and Port Hamilton Basins fading on twentieth century maps, bar a street sign and a carving on an Art Deco house on Lothian Road.

Maggie Mackay

You won't remember the weatherman

who smiled and said
there wouldn't be a hurricane
but it might get blowy

or the rain whooshing
over the downs
to clatter our windows
and make your big brother
yelp in his sleep

or the gale that smashed
the fir trees on the rec
and whirled our rotary clothes line
until I thought it would fly

or how wet your dad's pyjamas got
when he ran out to save it
how we snuggled up in bed after
his hands on my belly

to feel you
turning and turning

Sharon Phillips

I'm not hoping for rescue at my age

He says, as we sit in the café on the harbour .
I know the kindest sea would break him in seconds

the wheeze of winter squeezing every breath
all flop and flounder coughed up on the next wave

Strangers would point, ask if he were driftwood
wreckage, the gist of a gull? I'd tell them

you were a tug, brimmed with salt washed yarns
huffing into harbour on the lap and lag of inflow

And there we'll be, all of us in the café, on the prom
waiting with each other, watching the wilful work of waves

at the tideline, the shadow and shine left behind
all they give, and all they take, and all they give.

Julie Elizabeth Griffiths

Flood warning

We climb the stairs, suspecting, while we sleep,
the inundating tide will creep above its banks
bringing reeds, and planks, and water-weeds,
branches torn from their moorings, blooms adrift,
borne floating in the gift of the rising river.

The sandbags, propped rotund against our doors,
a futility of sacking, soon soaked and full,
are breached, as fish are washed, gasping and flapping,
into gardens. The flood, now feasted and replete,
making a midnight Venice of these streets.

Judi Sutherland

In my water

If I am water more than I am anything else,
I will run, filter through, fill empty spaces.
My fluid will be the abundance, abandon
of me, my freedom. I will seep through,
surge and pool, let you trespass in me.
People can picnic at my edges, dangle
feet at the cool rim, watch fish jumping.
When I am ready, I may allow boating,
lovely couples drifting careless in punts.
I will drink myself, swallow, lick my lips
to find more of me. Let me flood, flow,
be the waterfall tumbling. If I am water
more than I am anything else, I want to
mix, feel entanglement, stir things up.
I am the chemistry, elemental property
essential to everything we need to be.
And if desiccation begins, drying out
our chances, I'll feel it in my water
that I should have stored some,
kept a little back. Water marks
will be the only evidence
I once dripped slowly;
drip, drip, drip,
to the last
drop.

Pat Edwards

Keeping out the cold

take the ruby scarf of sunrise,
wrap up endlessly
in its soft jacquard folds

crown your head in a hat of leaves
plucked from footways,
feel the faded heat of summer

imbibe a cup of fuzzy cocoa,
its swirling thermals
making you melt from within

unleash spice jars in the kitchen,
cinnamon and ginger,
wallow in the sniff and scent

fill a hot water bottle with ire,
wear it close against
your brushed pyjama sleeve

snuggle inside the bear hugs
of seeming strangers
who harbour no ill chill

and if all else fails, switch on
the cranky heating
and freeze to bloody icicles

Linda Marshall

Learning

I didn't know Marshall's first name
because we didn't use them;
but all thirty-two of us in the class

were friends. You could say we were a team
but we didn't play different positions:
we were interchangeable, protecting each other

from a range of common fears: the bigger boys,
the teachers, the playground, the gristly lunches,
the bus home, the swimming periods, the unknown.

We were in everything together
so when Mr Phillips, who taught by taunt,
stood us at the deep end of the pool and barked

Jump in, and a ducking if you can't crawl a length,
there was no backing out. But we all knew
that Marshall couldn't swim.

I'd learned from Mr Davies at Drummond Road,
so I'd felt how it was to be thrown in to survive
or sink.

William Coniston

Lithium

Get me some water, love

A robe is clutched, pink and sagging.
White tube full-stopped in red, sucked on,
surrendered briefly to the toast plate.

She reaches for the brown bottle,
Tips out two white discs, thrown quickly
down with water she seemed to despise.

I'd imagine the discs whooshing, white-water
rafting down, sinking at the bottom into a pool,
dark like Ibbeth Peril from our school trip.

A pause, then up they bob before splitting
apart into specs flying off on a mission
to damp down her mad words, mad ideas.

Or the water would wash down capsules
that uncouple like shuttles, freeing
sparks to burn away the sticky gloom.

I'd tip water she left in my Venus fly-trap.
I tried hard to tend to it carefully.
It died anyway.

Debi Lyons

Melusine

There is too much of you, said everyone.
So she hid in her bath, floating
on bubbles and cocaine
and not much else.

You must be a model
for your daughters, said everyone.
So she gave up the high life, the high wire,
all the things that had made her.

We just don't think you're getting this,
said everyone. *You're too different.*
So she picked at her waist, found an edge,
and peeled scales away like rainbows.

Other quiet women come
from everywhere to the rocks,
bringing blankets and tea, words
like charms of protection. They sing.
They sing, rocking her,
careful not to touch the scar,
the bloody ridge her self has left.

Jennifer A. McGowan

Midsummer: dipping our toes in

Millpool-still at dawn, the sound waits
to be stirred. All day long, its depths are churned
by ferries, sailboats, liners; hulls tug
at the water, mulling it over, and over,
plaiting then unravelling the slipstream
from ships, to craft new stories from old myths.
The seagulls know all its secrets; the cormorants
have learned every lesson from wash and wake,
and ducks testify this fickle element
can stiffen in winter; clasp in ice
what once was fluid. A mirror to whim
of sky and wind the water shifts, skims,
threads itself with brightness, and,
as the day veers towards dusk, flicks the switch
on scintillating specks – stars, perhaps,
that fell during the brief night,
but refused to sink.
This watery world washes our wounds,
leaches tears into its brackish flow.
We are not new to passion's tidal pull,
but this is a novitiate of sorts,
which needs us both to navigate a route
somewhere; and you, the helmsman
in this northern sea. Board me, steer me,
free me from the frozen years.
Hold me, thaw me, see me flow.

Hannah Stone

Dunwich: February 2020

a jersey-cream moon
hangs bright all day
the sky vast indifferent

sun gold-plates the pools
the sea leaves between heaped flints
salt marsh lichen spikes

redshanks potter through the sunset blaze
scatter cloud-twists
into the held breath of evening

unseasonal sun
has seduced daffodils
even tulip tips

from the banked sea defences
the spring tide rumbles
gnaws at the cliffs

the drowned town
cries out

Sue Butler

My friend's cousin

Swept from rocks
by an Atlantic storm surge
within sight of Skellig Michael.

Suicide, the priest said, a mortal sin.
He shall never see the Face of God.

Buried in the cillin with unbaptised infants,
stillborn babies and shipwrecked sailors.

Unconsecrated ground.
No requiem, no holy blessings.

But his memorial
is in the radiance of light
refracted through spindrift,
a whale backed arc
of blue molten glass

and in that red-gold moment
when the sun drops
into the sea.

Sue Mackrell

Naiad

Diana Nyad, reaching shore,
was swollen beyond recognition.
The ocean insists on itself,
bypasses skin.
It is said
if you accept this
you will never drown.

This is a lie.
The ocean takes what it takes
asks only for love
drags it under.

Jennifer A. McGowan

By-sea

The water in my mother's tap was hard;
lime furred my throat, a kettle spout.
I took slow swallows and waited.

Brine scalded my blood as I fought waves
with red thighs, ploughed the numb water.
Later, rubbed raw with sand towels.

A tender touch was there at night,
in her piano-playing, her fingers
as she shampooed my hair.

This is enough to remember.

Ali Murphy

Narrowboat

Sedately we shuttle
through a warp of bridges
dragging a catch
of woken butterflies.

Kingfishers know us:
the jawless whale,
cutter of mare's tail,
crusher of buttercups.

Mallards gossip
of our coming and going
as they ride the lift
of our silk-brown ripples.

We rest under willows,
wallow beside
root-caves a-wash
with the water's music.

Saga of bovine
dreams, we form
a knot on the thread
of their blissful days.

And we weave our own dreams:
wrap ourselves nightly
in green, green folds
of the day's long tapestry.

Damaris West

North Yorkshire steam train

Some memories are sounds.
The chug of the steam engine
straining up the incline
towards Grosmont.
Listening to the wheels slip.
All that metal, powered by water.
We love it, seek it out on bank holidays,
take our children to see the beast,
smell the smoke,
and listen to that sound
of steam pushing pistons.

Tonnie Richmond

Pond life

Within a day the dragonflies came back
with a flirt of skirts and coiling tongues.
Wings touched dainty down on dredgings
black as tar, left glooping on the path.

I'd emptied out the muck of years
and found the fish I didn't know about.
He showed his evil pewter curves
when leaf-slime surfaced in the shallows.

As unexpected as piranha, that fish
ate my frogspawn, cruising, shark-like
in my own Sargasso sea.
I left the bastard in the sun to boil.

Kathy Gee

On Durham Heritage Coast

Gulls and crows loop around Seaham's striped
black and white lighthouse, as if drawn
by pit-shaft pulleys, clanking and screeching.

Wilting flowers die where they're tacked –
next to love notes on the wooden barriers between
earth, air and falling into the saddest depths,

always only a breath and footstep away.
Shadows continue their southwards taunt and dare
as the coastline sharpens to a jagged ripple

of storm-struck cliffs, bristled edges and more steep drops.
At Easington Colliery summit, I inhale another darkness,
and look out to a sea that the sun has silvered

to a pick blade un-blunted by coal. The path leads
down, but flanked these days by grass shallows,
bobbing butterflies and leaf-sailed wildlife pools.

An old man stops me. Leaning into his stick's slant,
he shares how some grew rich on the mix
of land and water, mining and hauling.

He doesn't mention the lost lives. His hands shake
with the weight of his words but his eyes are as blue
and lit as today's sky, blowing a different freight onwards.

I hike past Blackhall Rocks' rust-coloured stones
to the pebbled gold of Crimdon beach. Ghostly swirls
of dry sand rush to meet the waves, which break

into feathers of spray, flashing brief rainbows.
Distant wind turbines slice through layers of cloud,
mist and changing weather as machinery used to hack

into hard seams: *Hutton, Low Main, Seven Quarter,*
gas, coking, steam... Though little terns nest
and breed here, their return each year is more hope

now than certainty. Sand ghosts funnel
through crumbling dunes. The wind hollers
like miners racing to beat the relentless tides.

Sarah James

The Rigger
after John Burnside

This cold fog over the water takes me back to a day we shared
one sodden November. I was so naive I thought you really
loved me because you liked to stroke my hair. It was a shame
you weren't taller but I liked that you were strong and could
lift me off my feet without straining. You were quick and
agile, smart as a monkey, even though your face had deep
lines. Once you'd been a sailor and you could still hold a
room with a young man's risque sea tales but now you
worked the docks scaling cranes and containers and lived in
a high rise council flat. I went there once. It was bleak and
bare like a woman might have just moved on. I remember
this one day, though. The ferry to Gravesend. On the
windswept deck you pulled me closer. River fog rolled in,
settled on my lashes, closing my eyes to your kiss. What with
the engine chugging and the water being choppy, I felt
nauseous from a bit too much vodka. Later, you thanked me
for giving you my body. I was fifteen. You, forty-two.

Abigail Ottley

Painting the Saltmarsh

i.

this tideway is a palette
    dilute of seawashed mud
    slick of green weed
    shiny hint of flint
    bullying neon of buoys
        not yet scoured by sunlight

the creek is slow sludgy
        samphire dull at its poorly sewn edges
what is mud? silt or swamp riverbed or puddle?
    this mud is brim with tiny corpses
        ghost crabs crushed shells

ii.

did Turner ever paint the slip and shift of mud?
        Perhaps he only saw stories in sunset   fire
wounded warships the leached beauty of early mornings
        there are wrecks here too broken humble strays
they are not the Temeraire
        crowds clapping her final voyage
the ravaged celebrity of her hull

Turner's Margate is soft smiling vowels pale chalk-fed seas
what would his ratio be of marsh to sky, one to three?
skies so vast so sublime we tame them with dome or vault
how would Turner interpret the word *Blakeney*
in his mouth?   hard as a chestnut black promontory
where the clouds close like a lid
                             Sue Burge

Pause for breath

Away from intrusive tides -
in an in-between decade
the dock draws a long breath,
a sigh of sunlit contentment.
Behind a century of hooks, grappling irons,
to come a future of narcistic gentrification,
this glorious pause creates gold in the evening.

The dock basin, long since,
a scooped-out pool, is still;
in the Saturday evening, six o'clock,
the sculler balanced on the water
bends his powerful back
makes a muscular shape
energy coiled, but no ripples
on the liquid mirror;

the scull slides across
the tranquil plane,
no friction, no flurry,
with the swans
the docks only companion,
rhythm and harmony,
the song of the abandoned docks
before we come again with our busy purposes.

Colin Day

Portrait of water – *Blea Tarn – Cumbria*

A sable brush
slides   slant
    rain
      stipples
        the surface
          a rush
            of starlings
                        shifts   water   ruffles   sky
              from storm
        to sunlight
reeds   dart
        lamp black
                  becks
roll   Titanium white   Graphite grey
        bracken
              spills   copper
            screes   slip   gold
to   a   bowl
      of limestone moon
          pale and singing
                to passing clouds

perch jump
              pewter   melts   pours
          ore   and   rock   and   seams
ripple
        leaves
            scatter   skim   float
                          fells
fall   sink
                drown   *Kerry Darbishire*

Night in the river

The anticipation was of sharp currents,
surprises underfoot.
I was neither brave nor ready,
but the people under the darkening purple of late evening
were serene; slipping softly into the river's arms.
I followed.

We swam upstream.
Before, it was always downstream to the sea
but this was no ordinary congregation.
The sun was lost to the day, the moon about to show up.

The joy was fleeting before a city wall of old stone
forced us to the banks, to drip dark shadows onto steps,
seek places to gather and sit, find each other,
wonder at how we arrived here.

It was night when it began and then night returned.
The day was too short when the search for water resumed,
and the only thing left to do was swim.

Josie Moon

Rain bright days

These rain bright days,
between equinox and perihelion
white clouds stacked high
greater than the dreams
of Presidents and Emperors

I am alive between
Samhain and Beltane
when the wind scours the past,
recycling life, the elements renewed.

Where is the sorrow and the tears,
in red berries and wind-drift leaves?

Patrick Druggan

River of salt

Today I climbed a difficult hill,
in a desert, in the heat.
I carried a large rock, picked up
from *Oued Milh*– River of Salt.

Heavy with the weight of past,
I looked back at endless sand.
I placed my offering at the foot
of a tower nested by vultures.

I prayed and waited. Then it rained,
just a little. I opened my mouth
and precious drops dissolved salt rime
from my lips, from my eyes.

Its sweetness stayed like a song.
My tongue loosened
from the roof of my mouth
and my words were a libation
poured into the riverbed.

Rachael Clyne

Sea change

I wake up sour.
Strike out for the headland
where roaring spray fills fret smeared air.
Below me strands of kelp and wrack
writhe, helpless in a muddy sea.
Above, gulls keen – scavenging
the blighted wave washed crags
that threaten the dark and dour sky.

A sour day –
I turn for home.
Plod back across the cheerless heath
windblown and forlorn.
Leave the deserted shore for
wreckers' wraiths to plunder.

I wake up mellow.
Stroll toward the headland
through mists of velvet rain veiled heath
below a pearly blur of sky.
The air alive with the caw of gulls and
shushing surf as breakers glisten the rocks below –
leave sea filled pools of shifting shells
and stranded seaweed along the shore .

A mellow day.
I head for home –
alive with wind-buoyed joy
across a heath lit by beacons of gold gorse.
Behind, the deserted beach lies
waiting to be explored.   *Cate Anderson*

River watch

halt the day and
    watch the river slow
        to a broad meander
            taking it at a dreamy shuffle

        eddies swirl
        fish rise to poach
        gauche adolescent midges
        testing the season's
        temperature

    and willows
    barely there
    haunt the water's edge
    in early   cool
    spring air

        beyond willows
        and lambed fields
        a bank of blackthorn
        clouds distances with
        white promises of ends
        too far away

    below dangled feet
      the river cuts deep

        its sage-brown waters
           moving   moving on

     and supine river weeds

just submarine

tease the eye beneath
    the playful whirls

        of skittish fish
        and dancing eddies

    to darker waters
      nursing the river's
        true thrust

      meanders are for pausing only

Patricia Leighton

Riverish

The rain seeped through the pores of the earth,
came purling up again

marshland **river** saltings estuary muskeg
wetland morass mouth

polder pocosin waterway quag **river** mire fenland carr
fjord

bay **river** wash swale lagoon swamp holm salina pakihi

everglade aqueduct channel bog bayou slew watercourse

spillway **river** canal billabong course

drain rindle anabranch bourn gully crick ditch

rivulet branch freshet backwater

calvert rill tributary creek winterbourne **river**

gill voe stream brook

spring

Doryn Herbst

Rivers of Heaven
(After John Agard)

What was heaven like Enoch?
When your soul
landed at the gates,
did you have to show
immigration papers
or with entitled smile
pass native born
through the checkpoint,
and what happened to
the black borders
of your Christian heart.
When you sauntered
through the streets
with god gazing eyes,
saw *wide grinning,*
dreadlocked angels staring back,
did you cross to the other side
in primitive disgust
searching for your *decent,*
ordinary fellow Englishman.
When you patrolled the bounds
of a Heavenly Jerusalem,
Heard Bengali, Urdu and Swahili
catching on God's breath
did you wave your union jack
and petition St. Peter
to encourage *re-emigration.*
And when you came upon
the shores of Euphrates
surrounded by dark,
billowing spices
united with Albion bones;
did you blend
into the foaming river.   *Gary Akroyde*

91

Wish you were here
for my father

Whatever the weather
you'd charge headlong into the grey North Sea,
victorious in purple woollen trunks,
soaking up water like a baby's nappy.

Backstroke, blow-holing the brine, or
front crawling through the tea-brown swell.
Your natural habitat,
marked out by teenage scars from underwater wire
which ripped you
open like a can.

The war delivered you prematurely
into a Navy uniform and service for queen and country.
Floating you out across the sapphire sea,
into bloody battle.

All men together, sleeping, eating, shitting, singing.
Communal haircuts.
One barber, one style.
Corned beef for breakfast, lunch and tea.

This life on the ocean wave
This life which carved you, carried you
all the way from Brid to Australia
and to Victory on a sweltering tickertape day.

Sally Brown

Spate

Ankle-sucked in mud she slants over the beck,
steadies herself. A month of rain has filled the hills,
spilt over.

She lugs past twisted holly, where kids smoke weed
in the dry-boned church, dream under arched boughs.
Stones show the old boundary; a mark of times
when what you grew was what fed you,
when what was in your hands was all you had.

Beast-tracks lead to the water butt,
instinct driving them to take the easy way;
she follows, mapping the contours of place,
holding to soft hollows.

A rook flaps, flung to humming wires.
She skims the stile, out to the lane,
scrapes the land from her boots.

Liz McPherson

Send rain

We hold our breath before the forecast,
shut our eyes (don't want to see the yellow
map, the sunshine, north to south and east to west).
Forbidden hosepipes curl, like cast-off skins,
the outside tap, a rusted duct, a stoppered spring.
Above, a flying V of geese, discordant pilgrimage
casting cries like driftnets, trawling for rain.

Send rain.

Curtains pant through gaping windows,
trees crackle-glaze the earth with unquenched
roots, parched leaves applique crisp, brown lawns,
and twigs drop, quaking, snapping under fevered
mutterings of breeze, calligraphies of sticks,
logosyllables of drought - birds peck at stones -
and every day the sun shines carelessly.

Send rain.

Met-men and women, weary, apologetic,
squint and shrug, in-boxes full of scorn,
plaintive on-screen. *Don't shoot the messenger.*
The relentless sky burns on.
Long drowned villages emerge, a spire,
a chimney, lintels, sills and steps, timid little wrecks,
blinking in the glare – the reservoir a dribble in the dust.

Send rain.

Rain comes slowly at first, pinpricks popping dark,
silver bullets strafing windows, coins thrown in puddles,
cloudbursts of arrows from a sky like tarnished steel - rivers
crawl from their beds, wash through meadows, across lanes,
through streets and houses, crushing everything before them
sky moves over water on long grey rafts, the lidded eye
of moon, admires itself in cold, dark pools.
Underfoot a swamp.

Lesley Quayle

She is half in love with ink, which is pigment plus water

and half in love with the idea of
water. And half in love, too, the
maths hardly matters, with the
swirling patterns of colour she
sees every night not behind closed
lids but by the power of her
restless inner eye. She sees purple
and violet, rose pink and indigo,
green waves that undulate like
hillsides. Luminous, pulsating,
beating hearts, they fly like angels
or eagles. Sometimes she flies
with them, lodges on a star-arm,
sees the scope of all there is laid
out below. Other nights, while she
watches, the world spins on its
axis, a kaleidoscope of shifting
becoming. Like the patterned tube
of cardboard she was gifted once
at Christmas, not grasping how
much she was blessed. She sees
faces too. As if etched by fire,
they come swimming from the
well-spring of her consciousness.
Some of these faces are known to
her, all dead, lovely dears of her
days. Others are her Masters.
Their sad, clear eyes seek to
plumb her to find out her bottom.
Sometimes she will feel their

small weight shifting as they walk
so very lightly on her bones. Or
they brush her cheek with their
fingers of light, communicating
words mixed with water. Ink and
pigment, water and love. The
colour of energy is all.

Abigail Ottley

She went into the water

That's what the news report said
so I held my breath tight for her.
I worried for her, all fully clothed,
her shoes sludging with dark mud.
I felt the cold seepage, soft fabric
of her soaking against mature skin.
I gasped, took in dirty water, gulped
the current for her, tried to see her.
She went into the water, a trance
of her real self, drained, dissolved
like sugar in tea – the English cure.
Frogmen went into the water too.
They were looking for someone
amongst twisted shopping trolleys.
They searched for her, pushed by
strands of her, missed her by inches.
She floated into the news, became
a sad story, was eventually found
in ripples, in plastic bags, river silt.
I gave her the kiss of life, stranger
in my head, unresponsive, dead.

Pat Edwards

Standing on the ridge

Winter's bones lie in the fields.
Sky collects in pools between.
Sallow twigs burn yellow,
against this grey sky.

There is no present.
We lie to ourselves,
that we are frozen
momentarily in time,
a trick of language.

There is only past and future,
the constant ticking
of the telomeres,
calibrating a straight line,
counting down, down,
finite within the infinite.

This moment is past.

Patrick Druggan

The field runs through your body

salt swims through my veins.
You gather *vraic* from the beach,
tell me alganate grows prize-winning spuds.

I answer in merweed and froth-fresh,
tongued with salt on my lips.
I wish you would leave the sea to the sea.

You worry for the farmer who could be your Dad;
the land is tide soaked,
his tomato crop blasted in sand.

I tell you the run-off is bleeding brown
into blue. My bedrock is bitter,
we're killing the bay.

We sit on the shoreline together;
wedged further apart.

Sandra Noel

Sant Roma de Sau

When the rains failed this year in the drowned valley
the village rose up out of the water;
rebirthed, slippery in its caul of mud.
Everything under the flood, revealed.

Doña Eulalia visits the place:
the crumbled houses, the *Plaza Mayor*;
the stone church she knelt in as a young bride;
so well-preserved, that bell-tower.

She tells her great-niece how the people removed
down the mountain road to the market town.
No more gossip at the village pump,
just a turn of the tap and the water came!

The old folk say that the church bell peals
beneath the surface. The bellringer is the Devil.
But Eulalia sees there is no bell to toll.
It's lost, corroded, in the lake's black sump.

That night, she dreams that she stands in the shower.
Pouring on her head are stones and gravel.
Pebbles crush her bones, silt chokes her throat.
Water is finding its own level.

Judi Sutherland

The journey to Gaza,
Egypt 1964

is scrambled in my mind.
We stop in Alexandria.
Posh hotel with bell boys.
Thick Egyptian cotton
for a dress. White
with horizontal hieroglyphs.

A drive through desert.
Straight lonely road,
mirage oases.
Sand dust hazes the sky.
A random camel gallops
across the path.

A picnic by the red sea.
Heat—and headscarves.
Cartwheels on burning sand
and sea so salty it's hard
to dive to the bottom.

Planed, parched landscape.
The Gaza hotel:
three kidney shaped pools
and a beach to the sea.
In the distance
a mountain, a tree.

In restaurants
Egyptian women
wear gold and jewels.

A car exhaust
loud as a bomb
in the crowded street.

Jenny Robb

The coastline below your house has the beat of bitter in the shingle strand

I stride straight in slant light, swim into the bite.
Each lapping fold of my arms is all warp with no weft;
splinters ghost from my elbows.

A water demon writhes from the core of a wave,
gallops ashore in the shape of a stallion.
He paddles out to the deep with a man on his back;
wishing to steal his bride, he throws him to drown.

Cold slaps spur me towards Cheval Rock.
Envy broods in this stewing sea
where weed sucks and belches
around the remains of a petrified horse.

The same green coats the path to your house,
burrows under your skin.
You covet your brother's girl.

Sandra Noel

Swimming with dolphins

The Social Worker says it's so sad: Kenny and Steph
both passed away within a year of each other
and their flat is being cleared by Social Services.

The joiner's struggling with the lock.
There's a half-empty bottle of whiskey
by the side of Kenny's chair.
They had a view to die for:
the whole city spread out in front of them
in one wave of Kenny's glass.
The man who couldn't quite finish the Bells
smiles down at me from the walls
and so does Steph, whose ashes sit
on the sideboard surrounded by ceramic dolphins.

In one photo, she's surrounded by real ones,
rubbery grey-blue nose poking out
from under her arm, a wave knocking her off her feet.
The machinery in the lift shaft bangs

because life is a highrise: we rise and fall
past other people's lives, doors flicking past the window,
voices carrying from somewhere you can't place,
one woman's ceiling another guy's floor.

Which brings me back to Kenny and Steph
and the photos of them wearing the tartan Easter bonnets.
There are Glen Miller and Elvis CDs under the coffee table.
The Florida dolphins grin at me from out of a turquoise sea
that is now surrounding this block, the landing, filling the
lift shaft.

I'm wrong about everything.
Red kites shriek above the bus lanes.
Kenny's intercom goes off but they've got the wrong flat.
Sawdust is blowing onto the landing
and I can feel myself rising,
feel myself falling as the whole city is lifted up.
Steph puts on her bonnet. Kenny toasts me from his chair.

Ian Harker

The Severn

We stand exposed on the bank.
Our pale bodies jump out of a frame,
of dark green trees, a sudden summer sky,
one swan, as peaked and perfect as a dropped cloud.

We step into the sepia water.
Our limbs slowly disappearing,
as I think of the photographs we turned over this morning,
our dad, aunts, grandmother, grandfather, further back

and further.
The bend in the river we can no longer see.

Louise Warren

The river remembers

It has spent so long underground,
soil-sunk through limestone sieves

where it follows secret beds, soft paths
of least resistance, does not bother

itself with oxbow banks. No need
for fish, nor reeds, nor storm-made dams.

When the rain calls, it cannot refuse.
Must gather itself to rise once more, break

surface, find its earth-led form.
It knows the way – from beck to bridge

to culvert, its cool-liquid lava flow
unerring through the landscape.

Till it hits the drop where irate torrents
pour in peated fury to the bed below.

It comes, it covers, take no turn or stopping.
The river remembers what the stones can never know.

Penny Blackburn

The Tees

This loutish urban fox, slick-backed vulpes,
　　　　oblivious to your cares,
　　　　　　does not stop to lick your tears
　　　　　　even as you soothe your soul
　　　　　　　　on its boundaries.

It wends through marked spoors, roaming
　　　　　　towns, forests, fields, factories,
　　　　　　　marks its territories with pungency,
　　　　　industrial tinctures
　　　musk perfumes
　　　　stippled as whitebeam.

This slick-backed creature pushes on
　　　　　　　hungry.
　　　　It bites, bolts, snares and slinks its way,
scatters fertile silver tracks in summer
　　　　　　gristles its way through winter
　　　　　　　　- coating all things brown.
It tips trees, scavenges hillsides
　　　　　tumbles and tosses a thousand voices
creates the awe and liminal spaces, whispers or
roars as its mood changes.

It gives life and 　　　takes it.

This loutish urban fox, slick-backed vulpes,
　　　　　oblivious to your cares,
　　　　　　does not stop to lick your tears
　　　　　even as you soothe your soul
　　　on its boundaries.
　　　　　　　　　　　Catherine Walling

Turner's sketch of Kirkstall Abbey

At first my eye is drawn
to dark domes of stone, solid
columns, a sunlit day through
the open, broken window.
Within is standing water.

Wet has penetrated over
hundreds of years, the liturgy
has leached away. Connections
have loosened, edges crumbled,
interiors have been revealed.

Rain, chanting in the chamber,
has filled a stoup, spilled over,
washed away all human trace.
Here it is, pooled in the heart,
vault ventricles where no blood flows.

Lying at the base, liquid dissolves
arches into ripples, collects shadow
and luminescence. Cows dream
beside it, in a sanctum of slant sun.
It is still water.

Clare Wigzell

There you are again

on my patch at the headland's furthest point
where sea campion and thrift roister amid bright lichen,
salt-scoured twice a day. The Irish Sea smashes
its impatience to smithereens, suck and blow, scrape
and rattle. There you are —a pterosaur throw-back — wings
akimbo to dry, mouth agape at the thought of the next meal.

You weren't here yesterday, or
the day before, or weeks
before that. In the dark space
left when you vanished,
I touch an image of you, wait for
a call to tell me all is well.
Hope the stars will steer you
homeward. Each night
absence whittles that hope, until
all that remains is a cavern
full of wailing.

I watch a black dart skim feral breakers,
periscope along the surface. Hooked beak points
to the depths, sleek body rends the sea's blackness.
I hold my breath, count to thirty, scan the water
as far as the horizon.
There you are again – gulping down a fish, head first.

For a moment you eyeball me, then turn away.

Christian Donovan

Underwater

Drowned
     in the depths
          of your care home
chair.

You don't know me.

A Siren sings –
     she calls

your name.

Dadda, you echo; torpedoed
     to sunken

Lemurian
    shores—

Oh Dadda,
don't you know me?

Georgina Titmus

Unseen

We swam in Kirby creek one August night.
Moonlight came to find me across the water.
Robin said the moon had touched him too,
though there was no sign of it on the ripples
he sent out into the dark with each stroke.

When I walk through the woods at dawn,
low sunlight muddles through the leaves
and birdsong cleans my ears, but it's not me
for whom the birds sing. Sun and moon
find their way to every pair of eyes.

The unseen source that lights a neighbour's face
might be, perhaps, the same that dazzles you,
vicar, rabbi, priest, imam. Are you sure
that what you see is yours alone?

Sarah Mnatzaganian

Water pressure

the water drips
at 70 beats per minute
she is fed up
with not being listened to

now i have no choice
she is 24/7
and every night
she loudly fills
the washing-up bowl

i empty her
down the drain
she starts again
at once

she is preston new road
anti-fracker
she will be here
for as long
as it takes

she and i both know
she could
bring down
the kitchen ceiling

she is just one drop
but she could become
the flood
that changes
everything

Elspeth McLean

Wavelets

Six inches of pretending
to be strong and upright
curling coyly inwards
to lapse with a gasp
as supporting particles
collapse and a non-existent
mouth foams silver and white
and the shingle welcomes
whatever it brings,
slinging just the occasional
pebble as far as the force
of the crash can reach
up the sloping, shining,
retreating-tide-abandoned
beach.

Alwyn Marriage

Globes

Raindrops
Kissing plants as they settle
Falling life-givers, sustaining vibrant greens.
One sunbeam pierces cloud to
spotlight tiny insects, buzzing around
in its path.
                    Navigate the beam to
find a silver net, misted through a hedge.
Prey-less for now, the web ensnares a droplet.
Shimmering in the sunlight. Dazzling
my eyes.
                    Stopping me dead.
                                        Marvelling.
I look again, in awe of miniature beauty.
This simple brilliance encapsulates
my whole surrounding world.
                                        Perfectly caught
In every infinite detail. Every part
of every-thing is there. A global gem.
Tiny, clear precision.
                    Epiphany!

The universe is trapped within this sphere -
What if we exist inside another?

Could it be we're nested spheres in spheres, and
you are seeing me in your own bubble?
                                        Boakesey Closs

So you can love her

It started in the kitchen, a bucket
catching the steady drips. I count
the time between each drop. Five seconds.
Nothing a plumber can't fix until...

I don't know, he says, as if this can keep us dry
or prevent a flood. I tear apart our kitchen ceiling
and bathroom floor, pull up all our insulation
to find the source. Nothing.

How can water come from nothing? Water,
like me, is stubborn. Five seconds
turn into four...three...two...
one.

Our ghosts turn on all the taps at once. A waterfall.
The buckets can't hold it all, I try the old fish tank
and the saucepans. But it's too much, I can't empty
anything fast enough. The water level's rising.

I give up, gather all the photographs, scraps of love letters.
You play video games and sleep, take your sweet time
in the shower. You're so calm, so dry.
You don't notice we're living through a disaster.

Can't you see I'm treading water?
We shouldn't sink like this. I've known a hotel
to be sinkable: it fell into the water, a graceful catastrophe.
But I don't want us to be a catastrophe.

Maybe I am sinkable, too.
The door opens, lets out all the water,
lets out me. My perfume, my eyelashes on the pillow,
the toast I hadn't finished, is all washed away.

No trace of me. Between you and me,
I never existed. But you're still there,
living in a house, bone dry.
Grateful I'm gone.

Rachel Glass

Why swimming underwater is difficult

They went to assist, generations jostling,
heaving help heavily, running from other work.
Life-boat launched to raft and reach
those rock wrecked wolves of the sinister sea.

Judgement jutted sharp ricochets
in blinding waves that washed them
from point to piercing point, crashing
into splinters, that dispersed them down.

Depth drowned, wives who waited on the tideline
held space hopeful until it was certain; keened
weeks later when one bloated body beached.
Now it is said that he smiled, as if surely siren sung.

So, in chlorine fumed fakery, safe and sure
on cold ceramic tiles trodden by the fleet and fallen
I still cannot submit and submerge, allow myself to let go,
because slant shadows whisper, water is hungry.

Alison Jones

The Watcher

She walks backwards into the sea;
shingle gives ingress to her feet
before removing any word of her.

At her shoulder a scrappy halfmoon
of grey seals pause their morning hunt
to study this rum spectacle.

Her cotton shift loses a little pigment
day-by-day, so the dark blooms
are an unreadable cloud below the surface.

From the cliffs, you can see her, if you wish it.
And when the wind drops just enough,
seal-song will act like a balm.

Go to her now, she will send back your dead,
salvage your bedazzling treasures.
She can feel you are heartsore.

Helen Ivory, guest judge

Afterdrop

At six degrees you're in its thrall.
It is a mercy and you are fluid,
able to lift yourself, then fall. Lift
and fall.

You are everything you want to be:
strong, brave, seen. Yet so small
in here no one can find you,
however well they know you.

You float and it takes you, upstream
and back – further, if it wanted to.
And it's colder than you thought,
colder than the last time.

And when you're out, it's hard to see,
hard to stand. Hard to think.
Your hands and feet are back
but your core is a wide open space.

You can't remember why you're here,
or what it is you came for.

Gill Connors

Tregowris

I have no history here on the Lizard Peninsula but I'm
mapping one this morning, walking through wind-bent
trees, which have fashioned branched tunnels that filter
early sunlight, polka dot the narrow lanes, hemmed in by
hedgerows teeming with cow parsley, blue bells, forget me
nots, foxglove, common mallow, so tall these hedges, I
cannot see the ocean yet I know it's there from the salted
breeze, and hawfinches and stone chats flit and sing as I
walk into a clear view of the sea: a thin blue horizon above a
golden hay-made field, till I turn back towards the rented
cottage and the warm bed I left you in, as you knit another
row on a flourishing shawl that captures all the colours we
saw yesterday.

Mark Connors

Savour the earth

your senses welcome it
truthfully, effortlessly.

Post rain is perfume,
petrichor prolific and sweet
a post-storm treat.

Flavour of raw beet,
a kiss of soil to taste buds
blushed as energised blood.

Might of minerals,
in a quenching glass of water,
bound as brick to mortar.

Bristle of deciduous leaf,
roar of sea wave and thunder
hoot of midnight hunter.

Elation at glimpse of wildlife,
warmth and rejuvenation of sing-song
tears at fear of extinction.

Unfathomable gravity,
undulating tenacity of powerful tides,
inevitable erosion by time.   *Nick Steel*

Also published by Yaffle's Nest

The Worm in the Pheasant's Neck — Colin Day
Rear-view Mirror — Tonnie Richmond
Keep Taking Six Away From 100 — Tim Brookes
Rosa Brigante — Su Ryder
Liven Yourself Up — Sharon Phillips
Playing with Fire — Bill Fitzsimons
Mississippi Birdfeeder at Night — K.T Slattery
Spotlit Under Street Lamps — Sheila Jacob
Last Dance — Susan Castillo Street
Into the Under — Sandra Noel
The Ghosts of A and E — Nicky Carter
The Feral Parakeet — Elspeth McLean
Twenty Years and Counting — Jeffa Kay
Shivering in the Wind — Liz McPherson
Imprints — Peter Kay
Throwing Sugar on the Fire — Faye Marshall

Please go to Yaffle's Nest/Yaffle (yafflepress.co.uk) to purchase any of the above titles.